Whale shark

Bull shark

Basking shark

Tiger shark

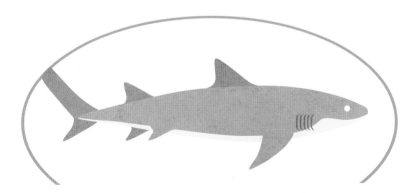

Lemon shark

Cookiecutter shark

To my amazing wife

ACKNOWLEDGMENT

Thank you to Dr. Melanie Hutchinson of the Shark Research Lab at the Hawai'i Institute
of Marine Biology for her expertise, attention to detail, and guidance.

Visit us on the Web! rhcbooks.com

Educators and librarians, for a variety of teaching tools, visit us at RHTeachersLibrarians.com

Library of Congress Cataloging-in-Publication Data
Names: Terranova, Michael-Paul, author.
Title: Chomp : a shark romp / Michael Paul.
Description: New York : Crown Books for Young Readers, [2019] | Audience: Age 2–5. | Audience: Grade: pre-school, excluding K.
Identifiers: LCCN 2018049001 | ISBN 978-1-5247-6702-0 (hc) | ISBN 978-1-5247-6704-4 (epub) | ISBN 978-1-5247-6703-7 (glb)
Subjects: LCSH: Sharks—Juvenile literature.
Classification: LCC QL638.9 .T465 2019 | DDC 597.3—dc23

MANUFACTURED IN CHINA   10 9 8 7 6 5 4 3   First Edition

CHOMP

A Shark Romp

Michael Paul

Crown Books for Young Readers

New York

There are many different types of sharks alive today.

FRILLED SHARK

BLUE SHARK

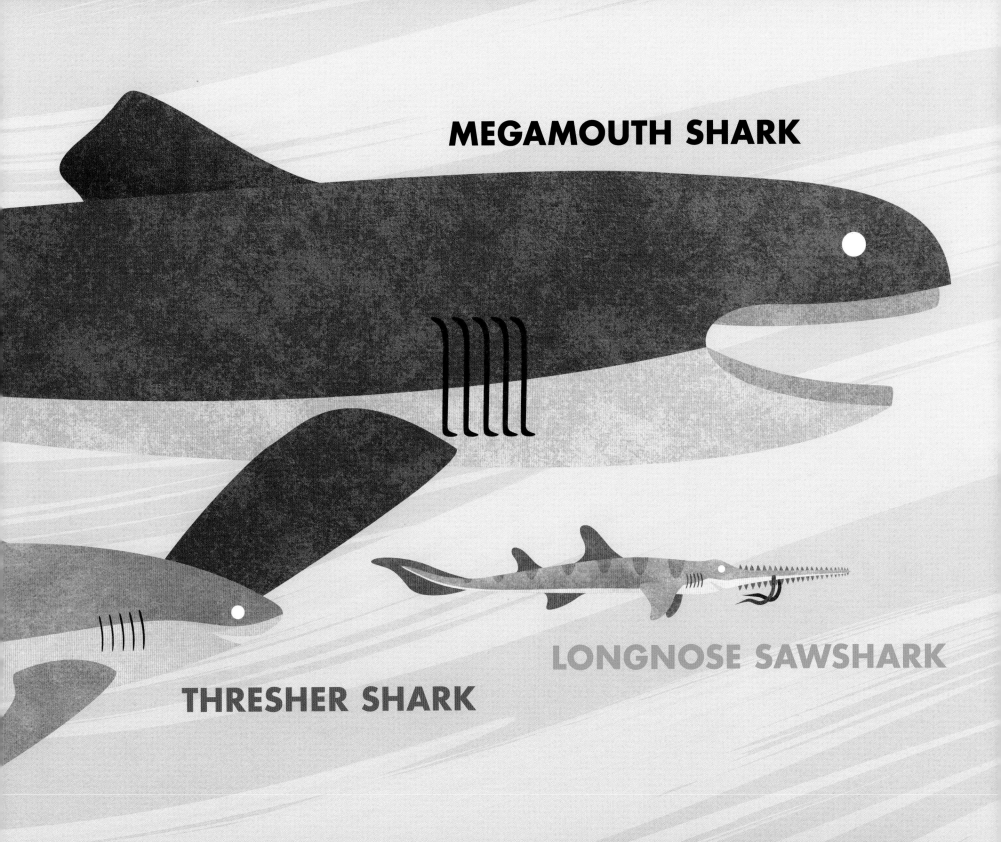

MEGAMOUTH SHARK

LONGNOSE SAWSHARK

THRESHER SHARK

Some sharks are gentle . . .

WHALE SHARK

but others are fierce.

BULL SHARK

Some sharks are picky eaters . . .

BASKING SHARK

while other sharks eat
almost anything.

CHOMP
PQR·567
SHARKS ARE GREAT
19

TIGER SHARK

There are sharks that live together . . .

LEMON SHARK

and sharks that live alone.

COOKIECUTTER SHARK

A few sharks like cold water . . .

GREENLAND SHARK

but most like it warmer.

GREAT HAMMERHEAD SHARK

Some sharks are hard to spot . . .

WOBBEGONG SHARK

while other sharks really shine.

LANTERN SHARK

There are sharks that are awake in the day . . .

SHORTFIN MAKO SHARK

and others that come out at night.

PYJAMA SHARK

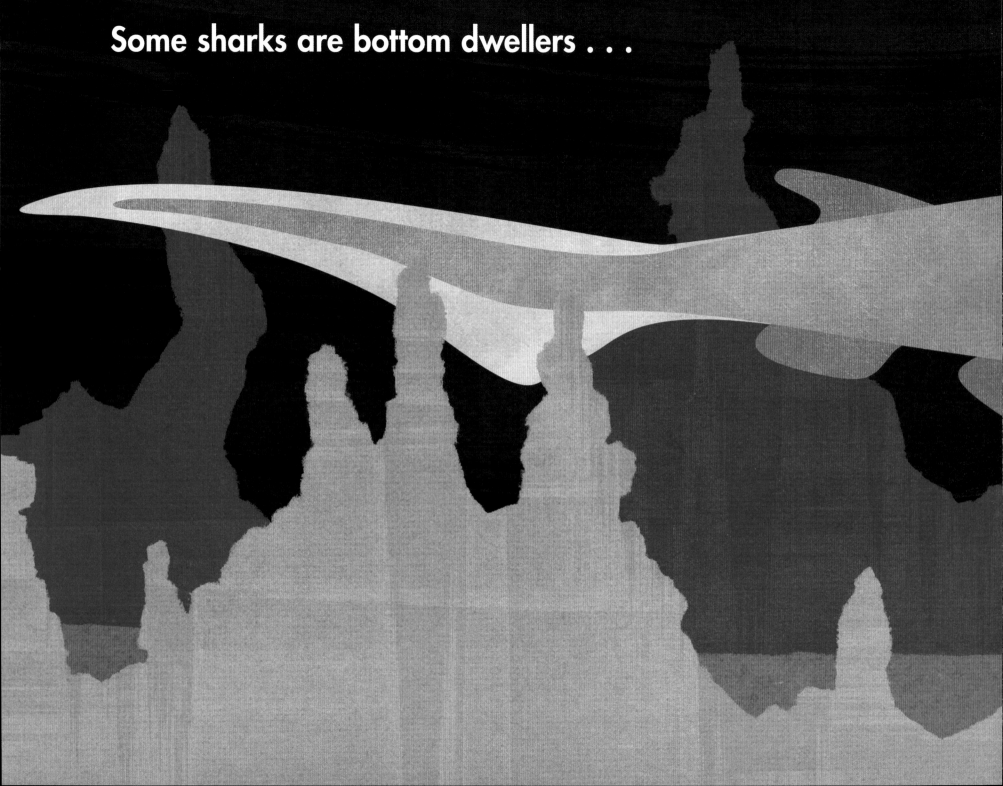

Some sharks are bottom dwellers . . .

GOBLIN SHARK

but other sharks are surface breakers.

GREAT WHITE SHARK

Today you can visit sharks up close at the aquarium.

LEOPARD SHARK   **ANGELSHARK**

PORT JACKSON SHARK   SANDBAR SHARK

Greenland shark

Great hammerhead shark

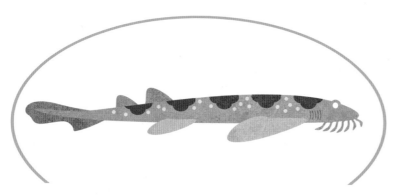

Wobbegong shark

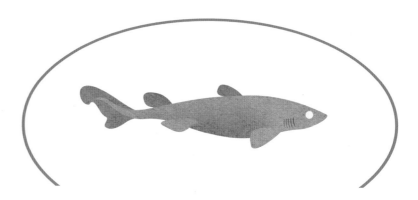

Lantern shark

Shortfin mako shark

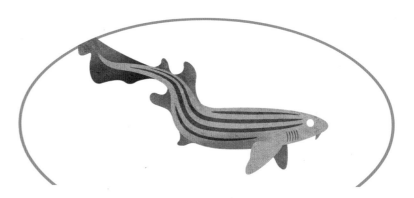

Pyjama shark